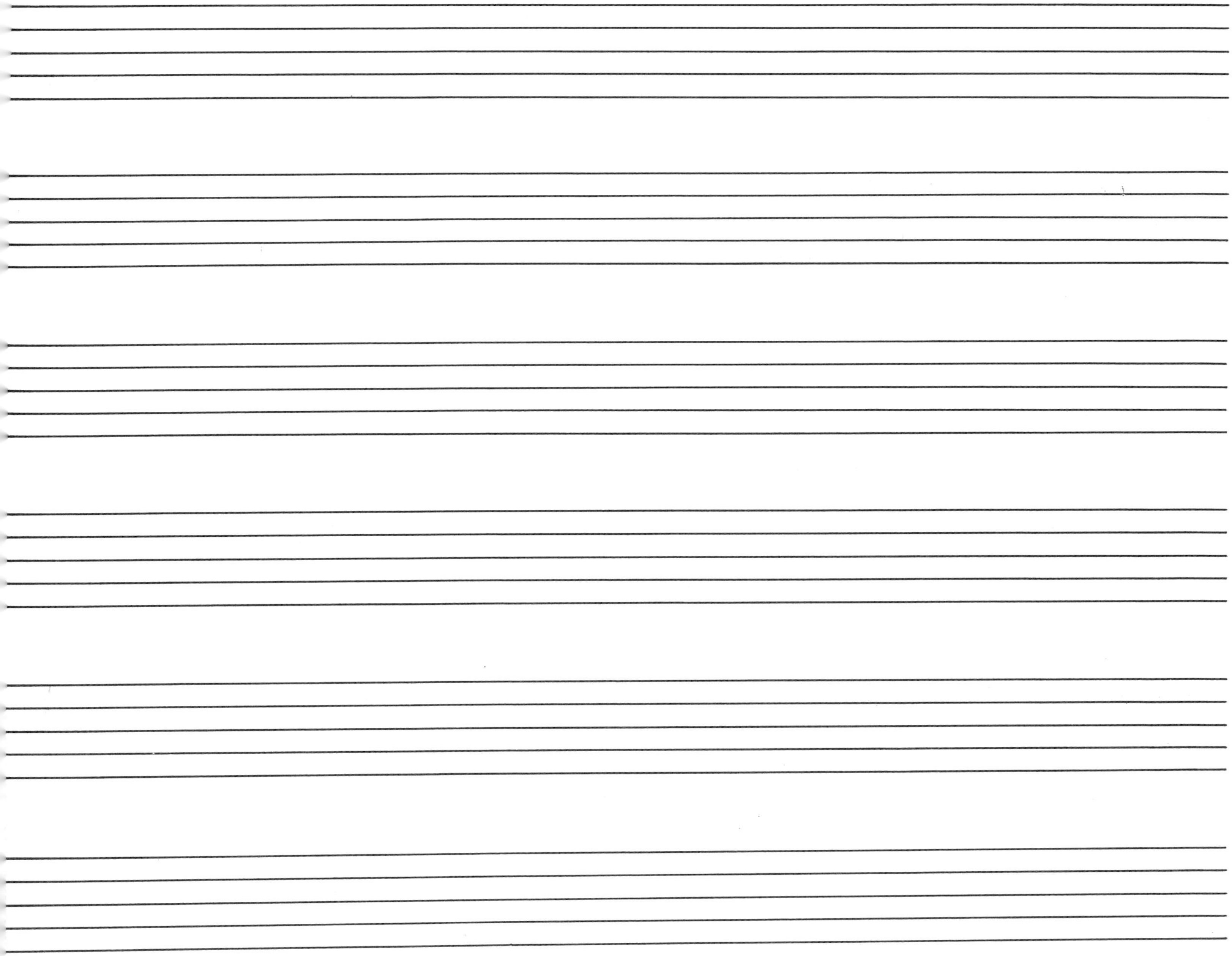

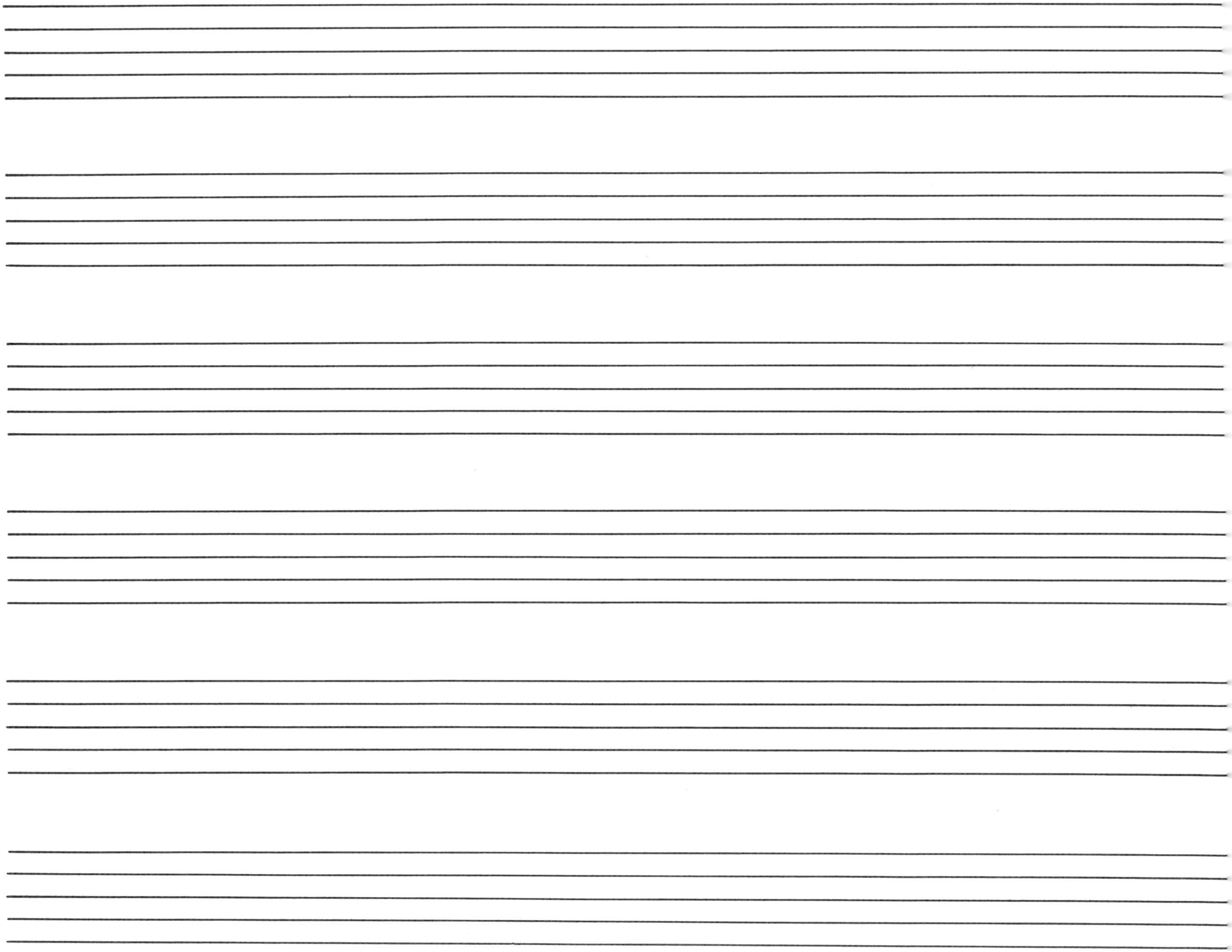

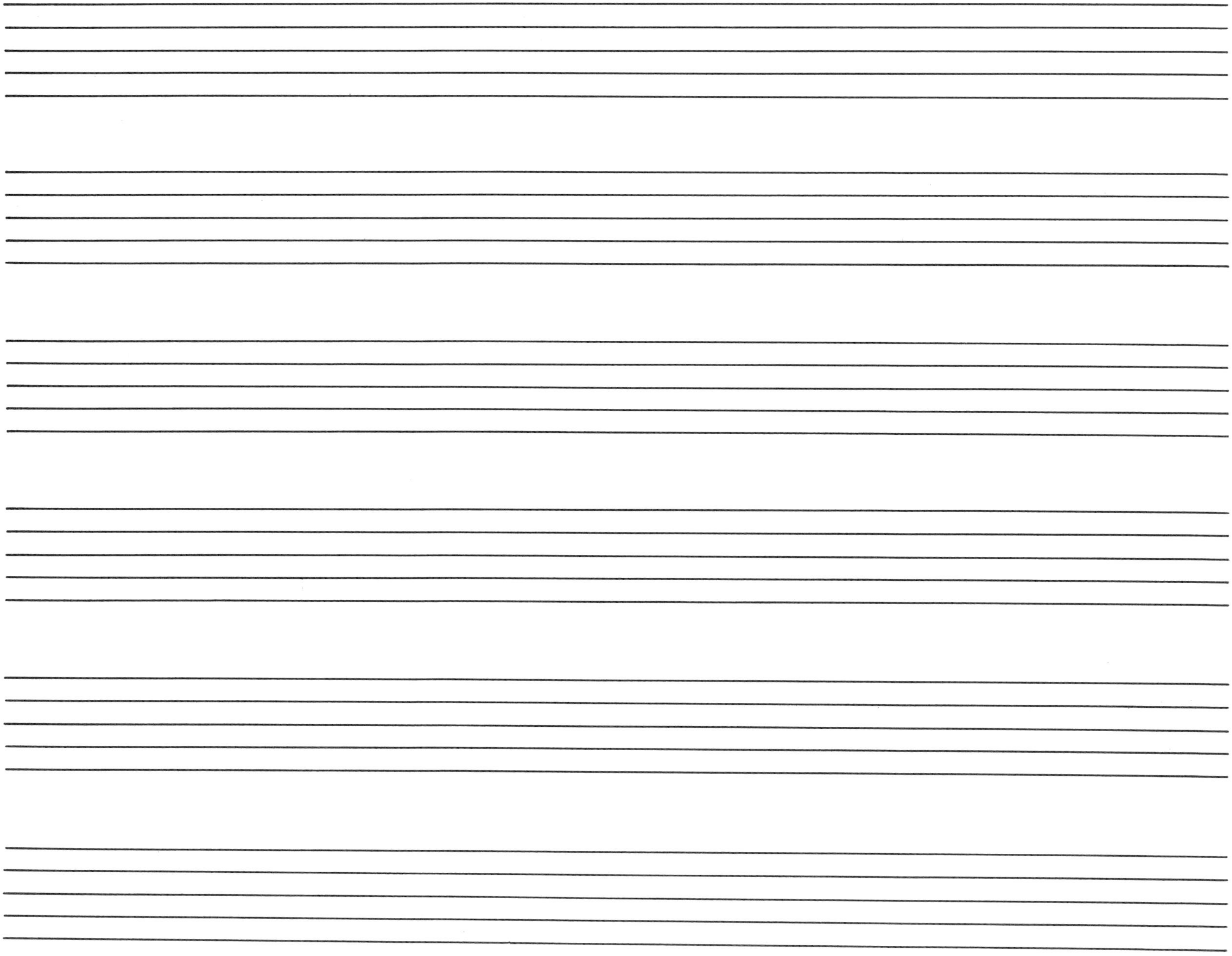

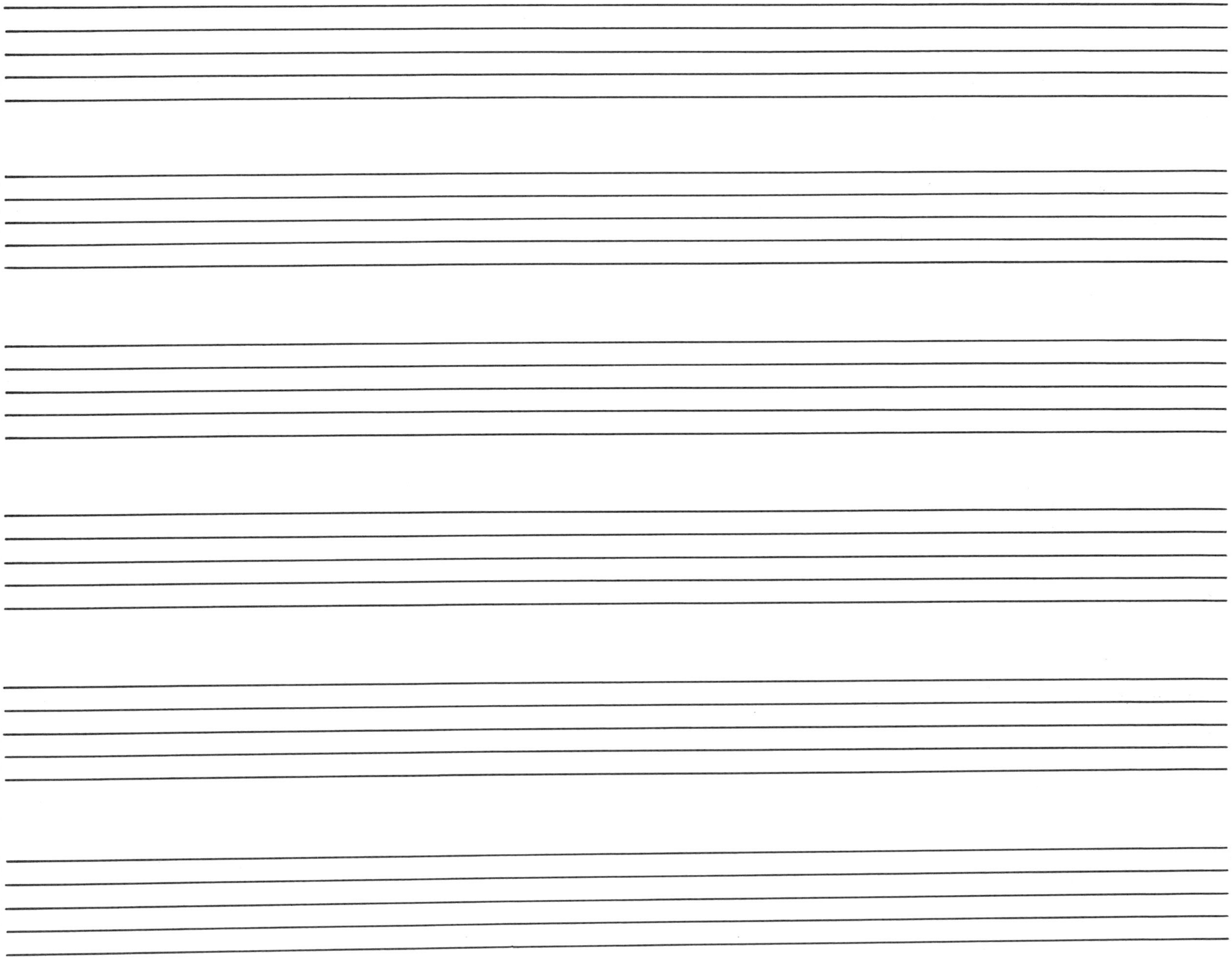

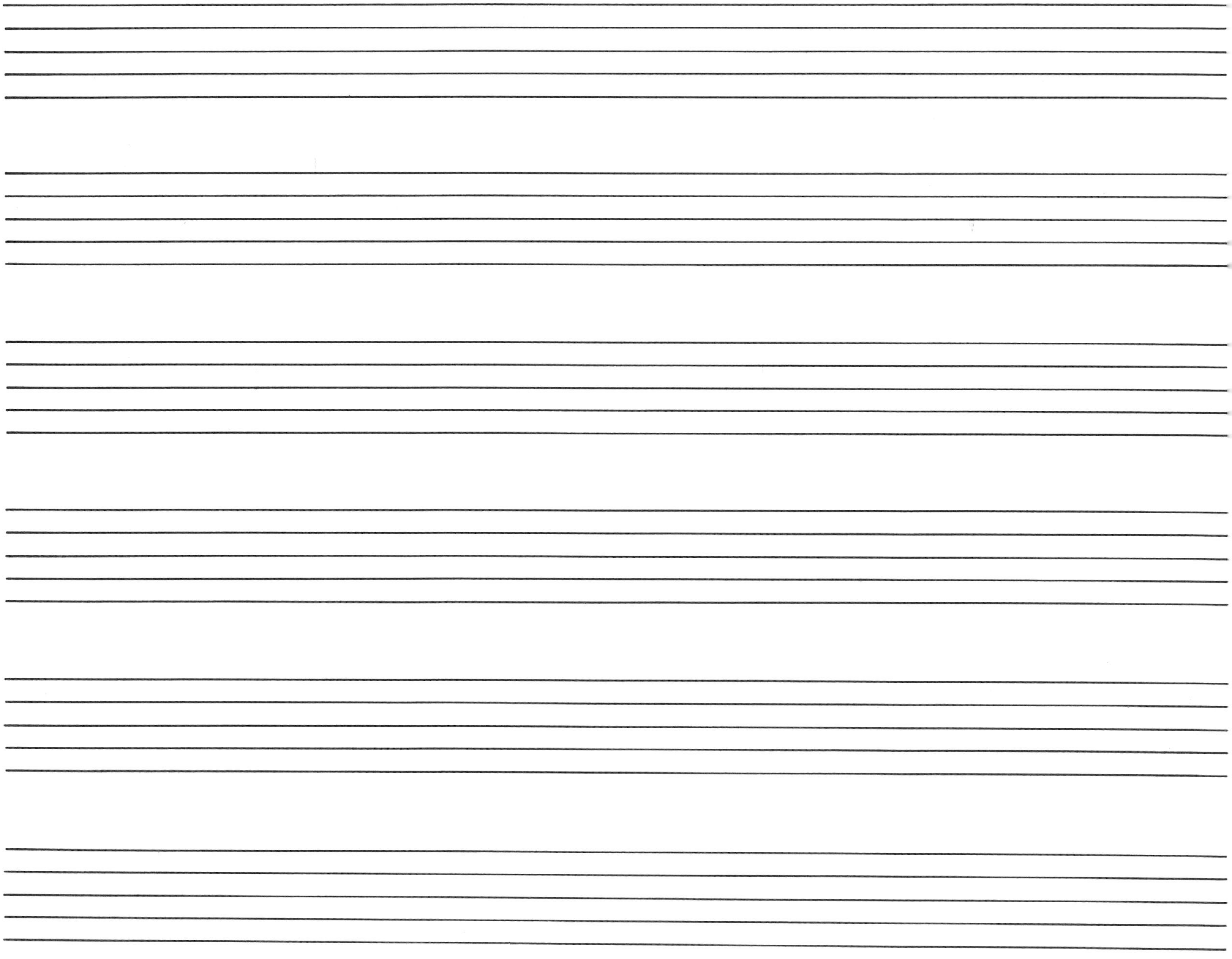

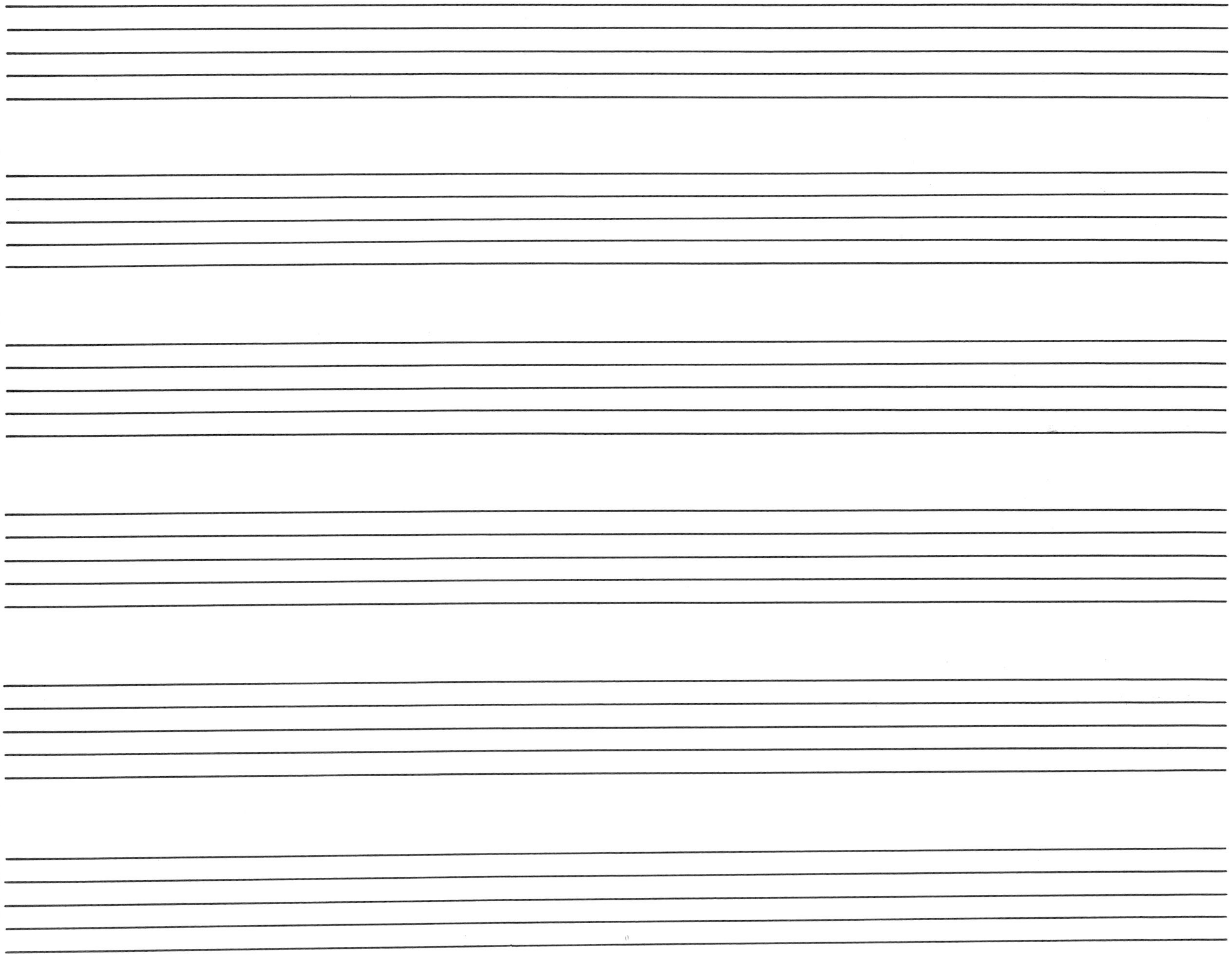

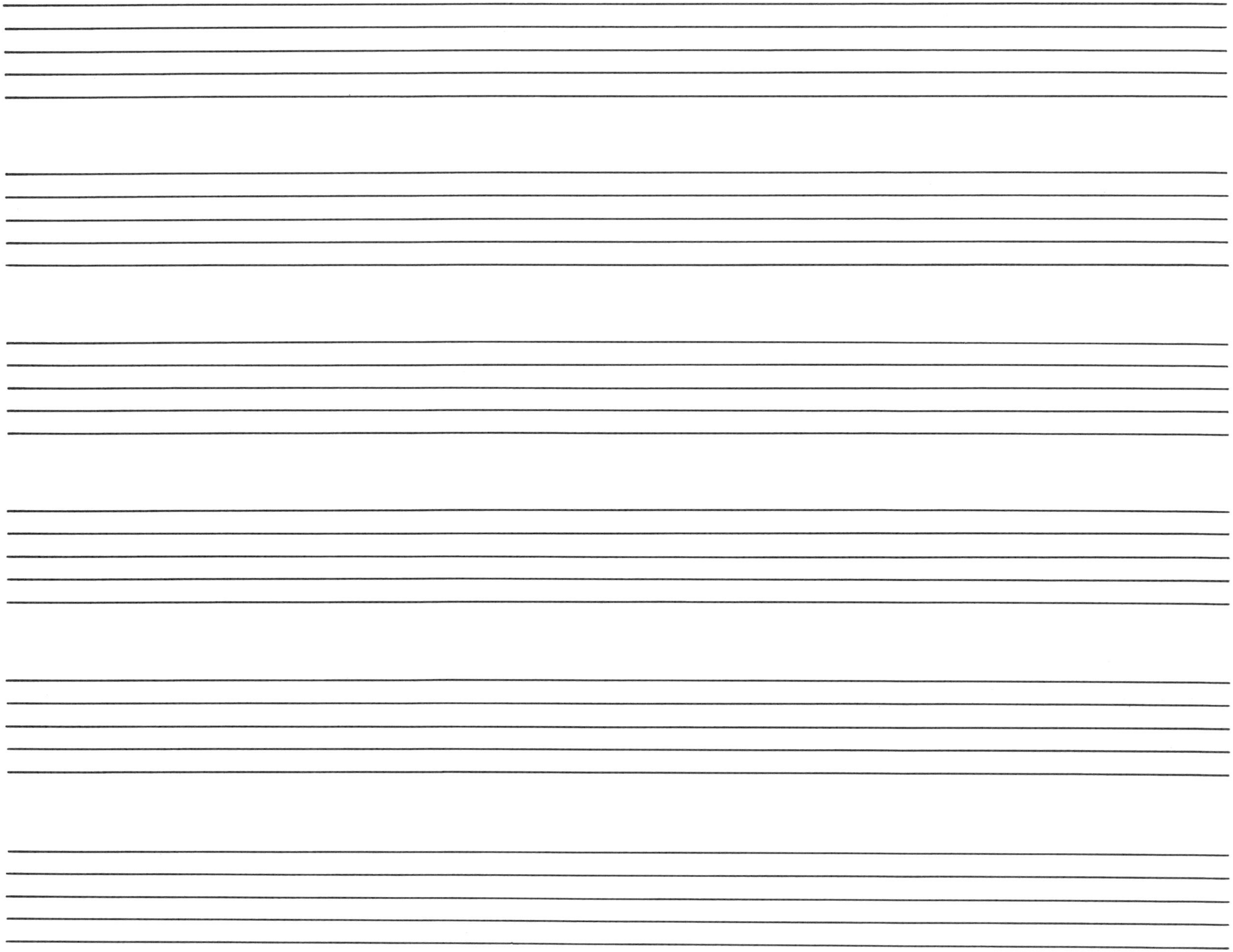

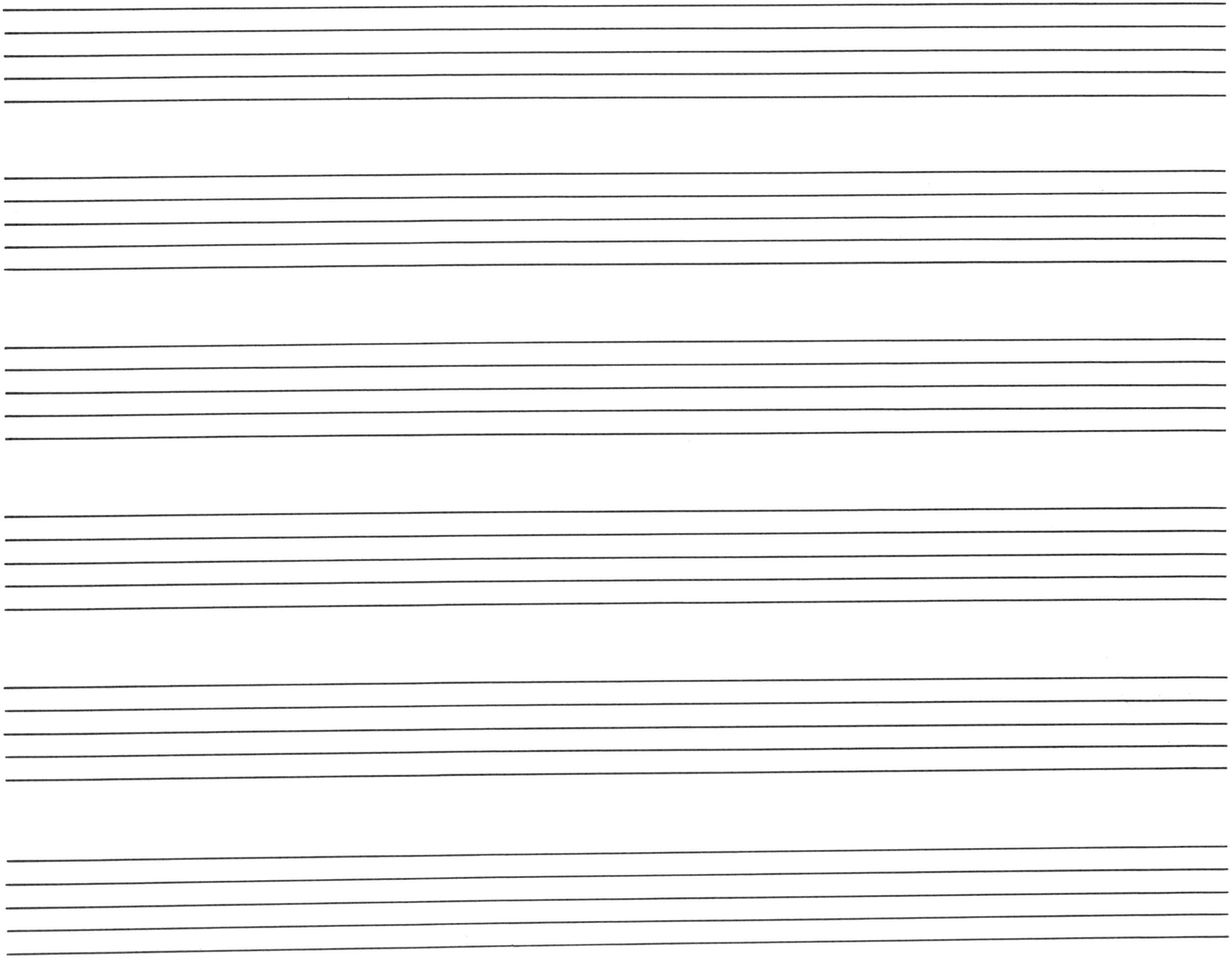

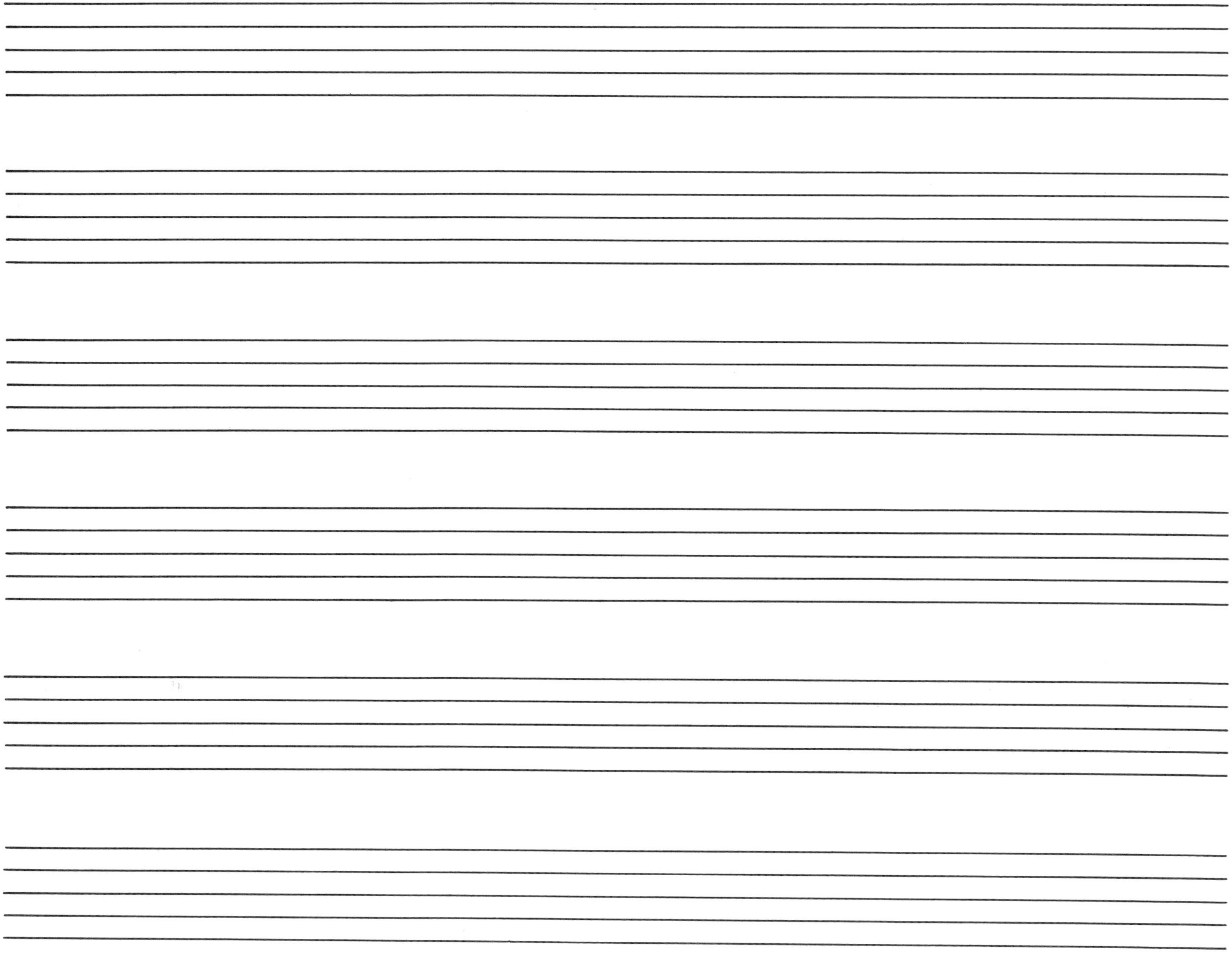

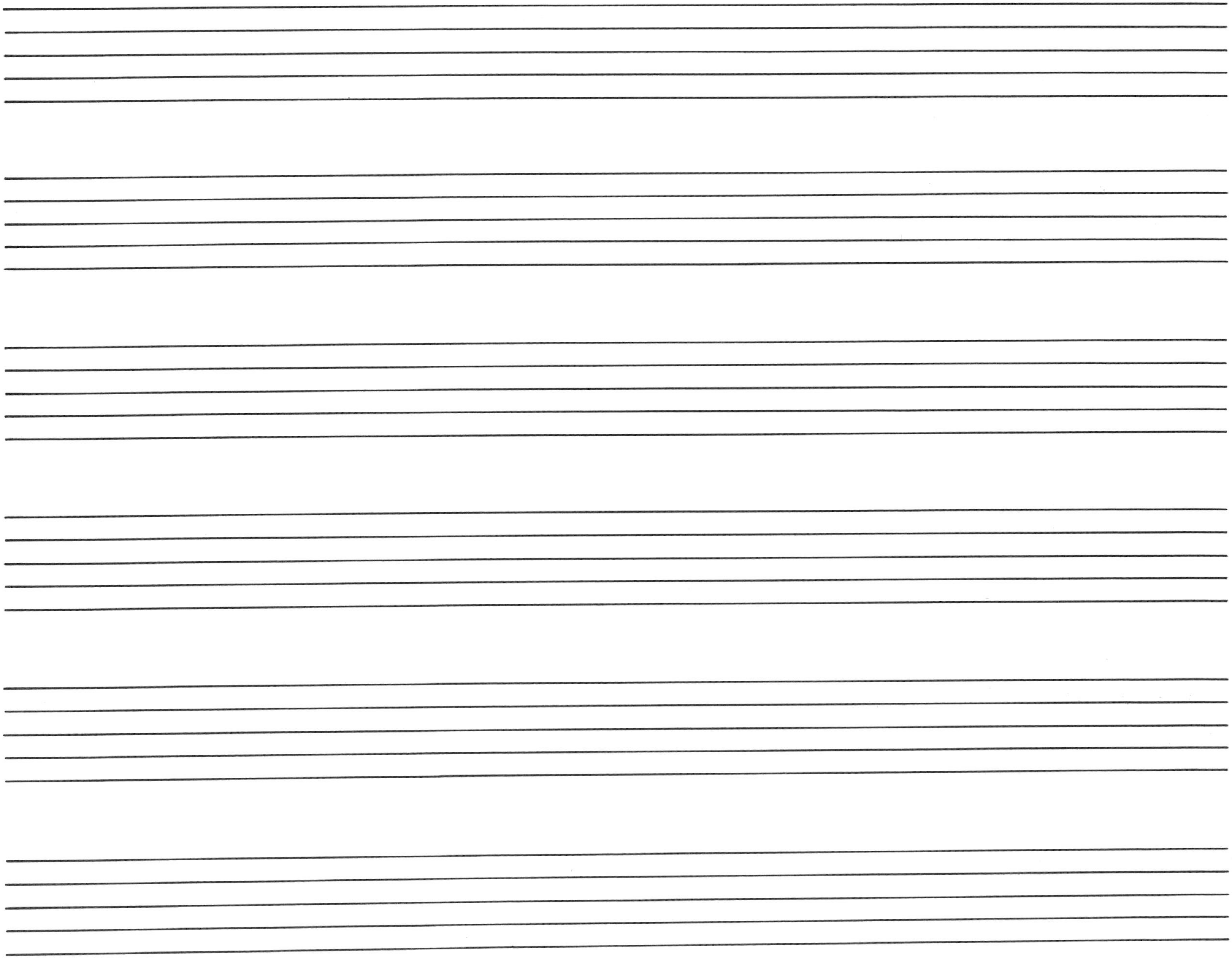

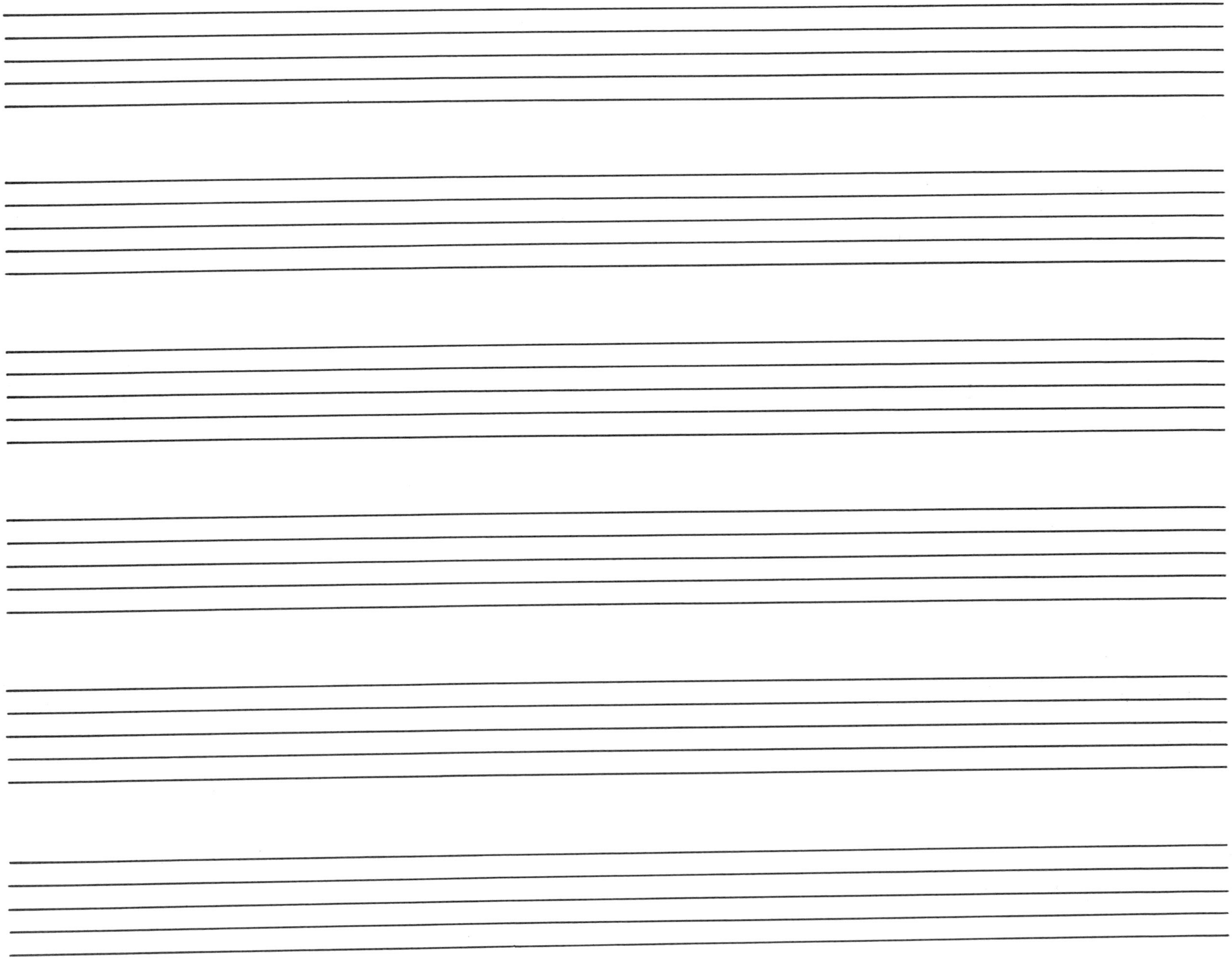

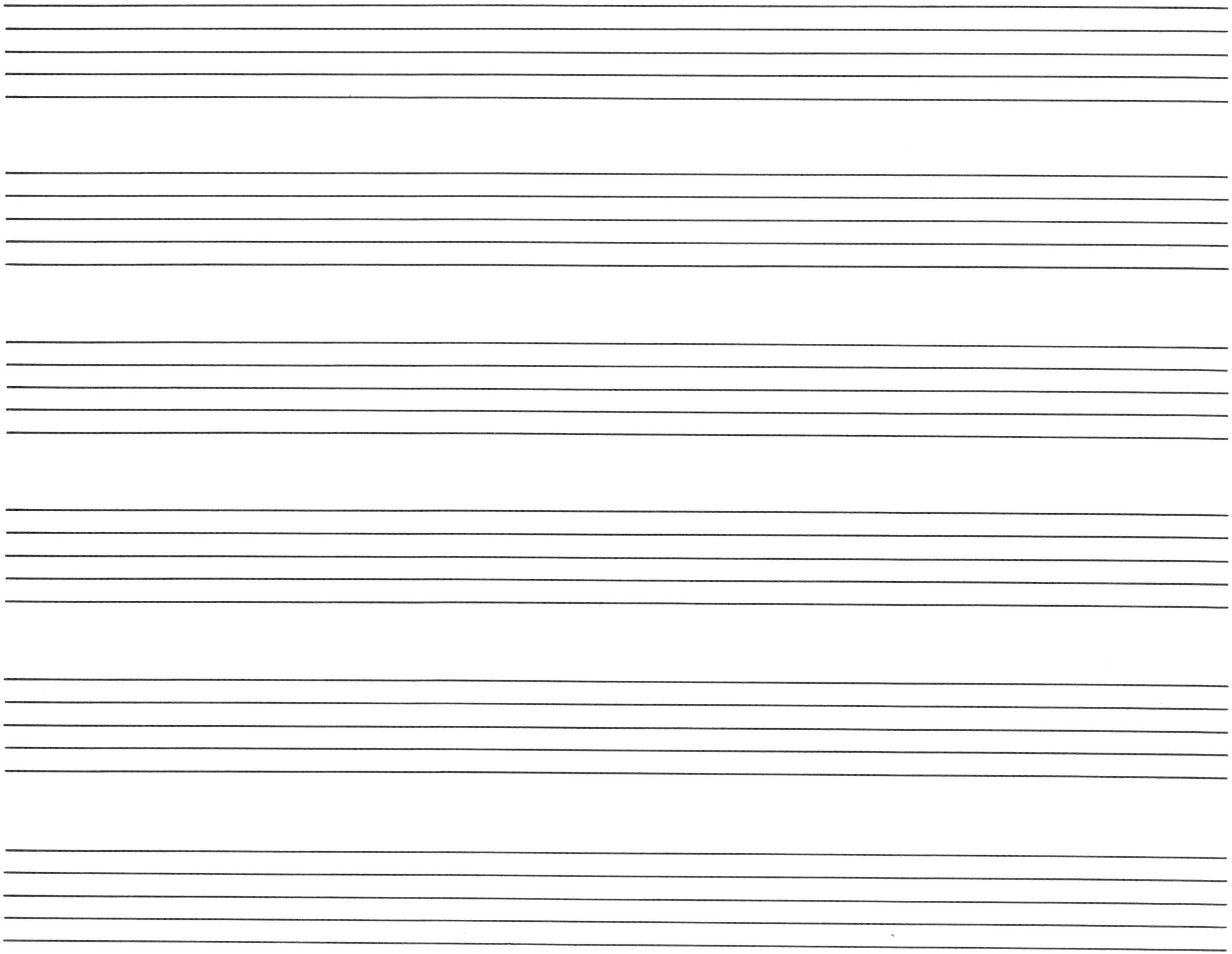

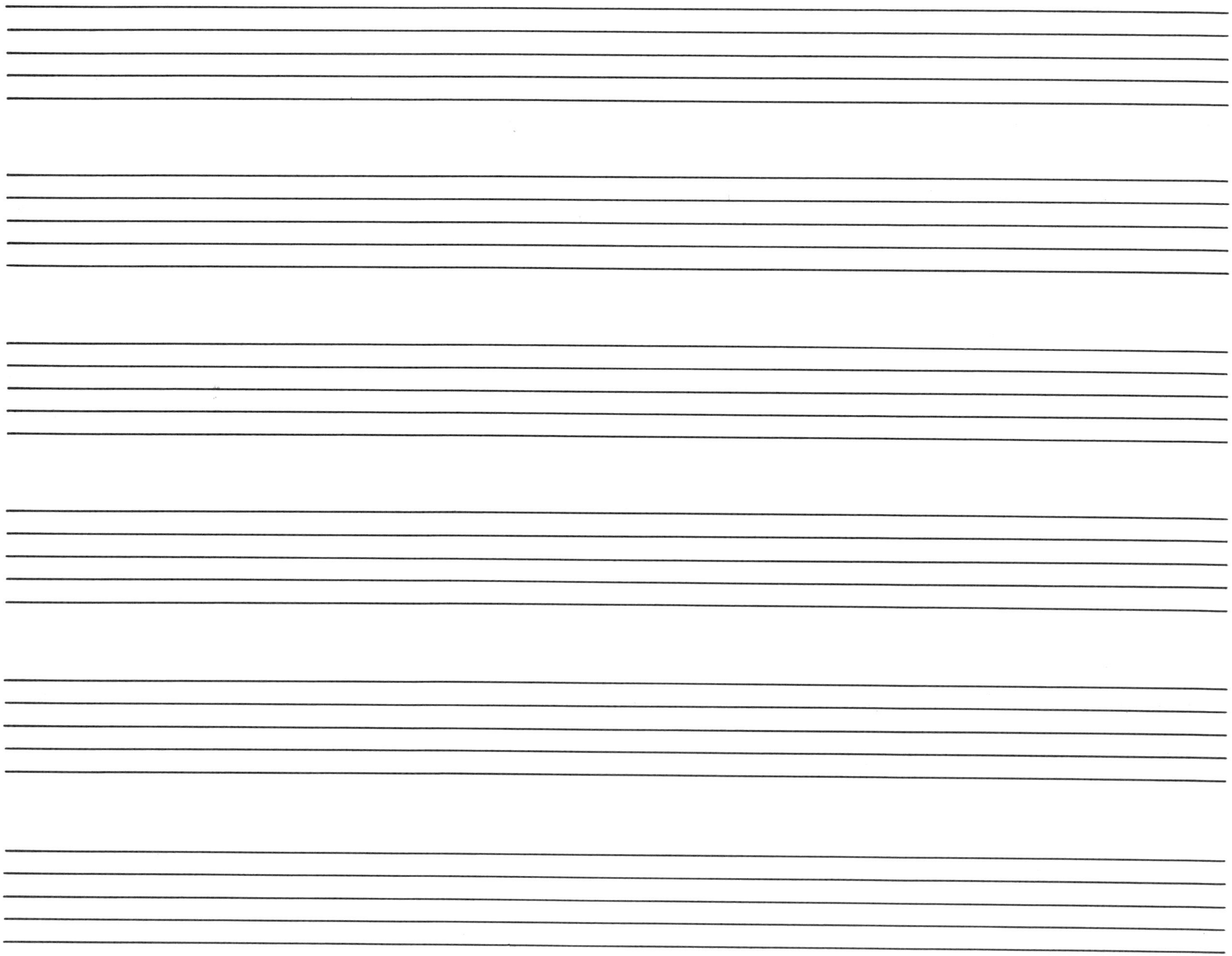

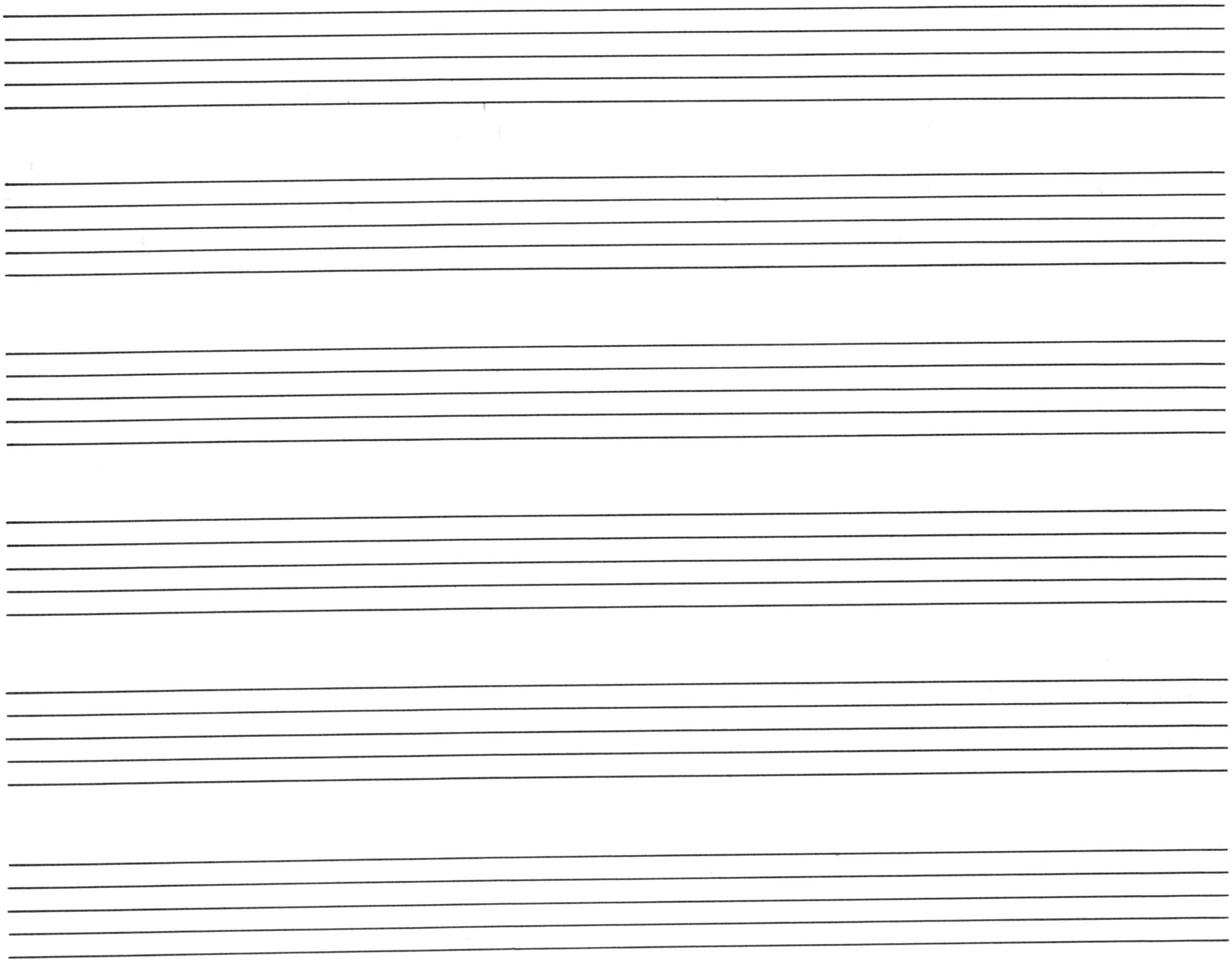

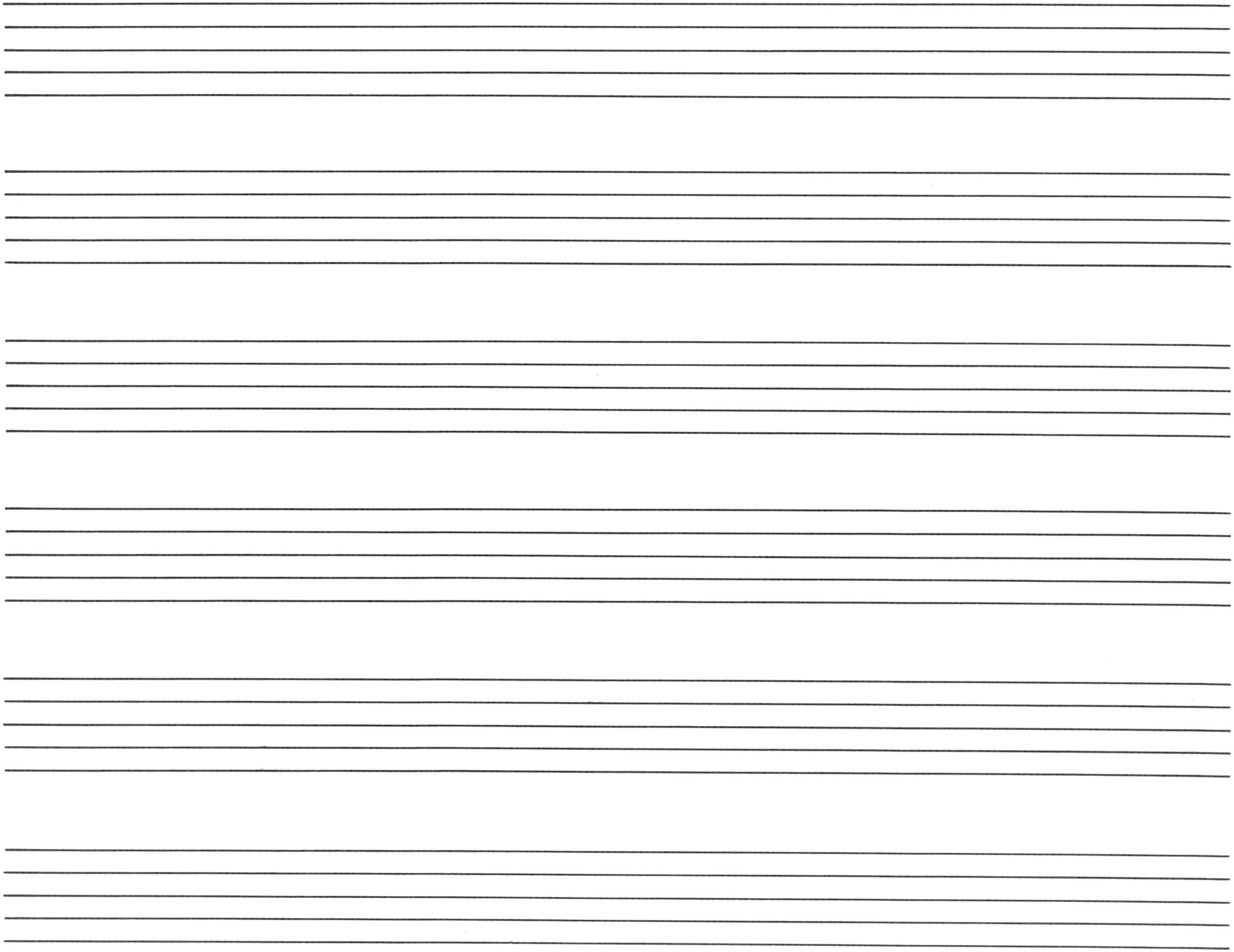

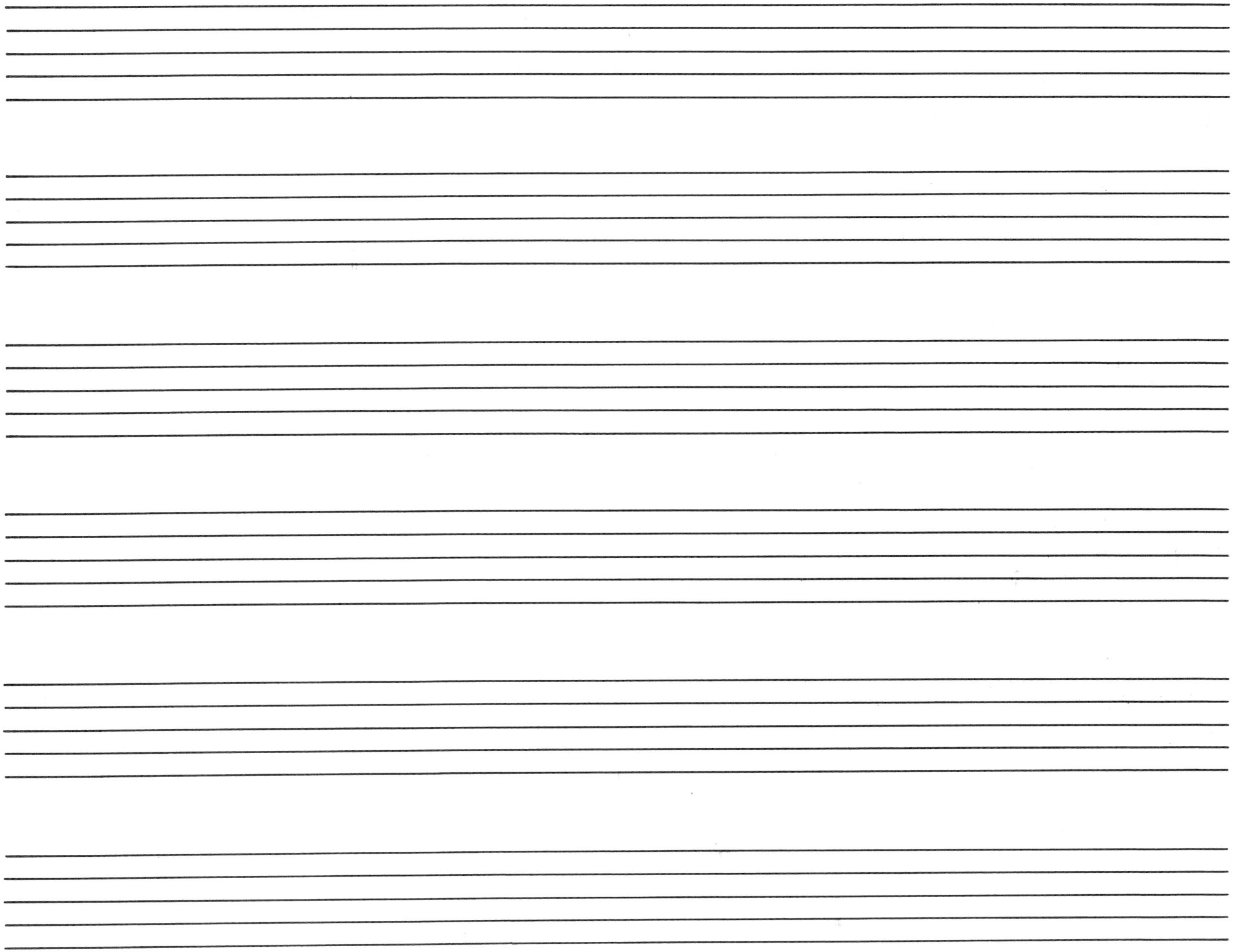

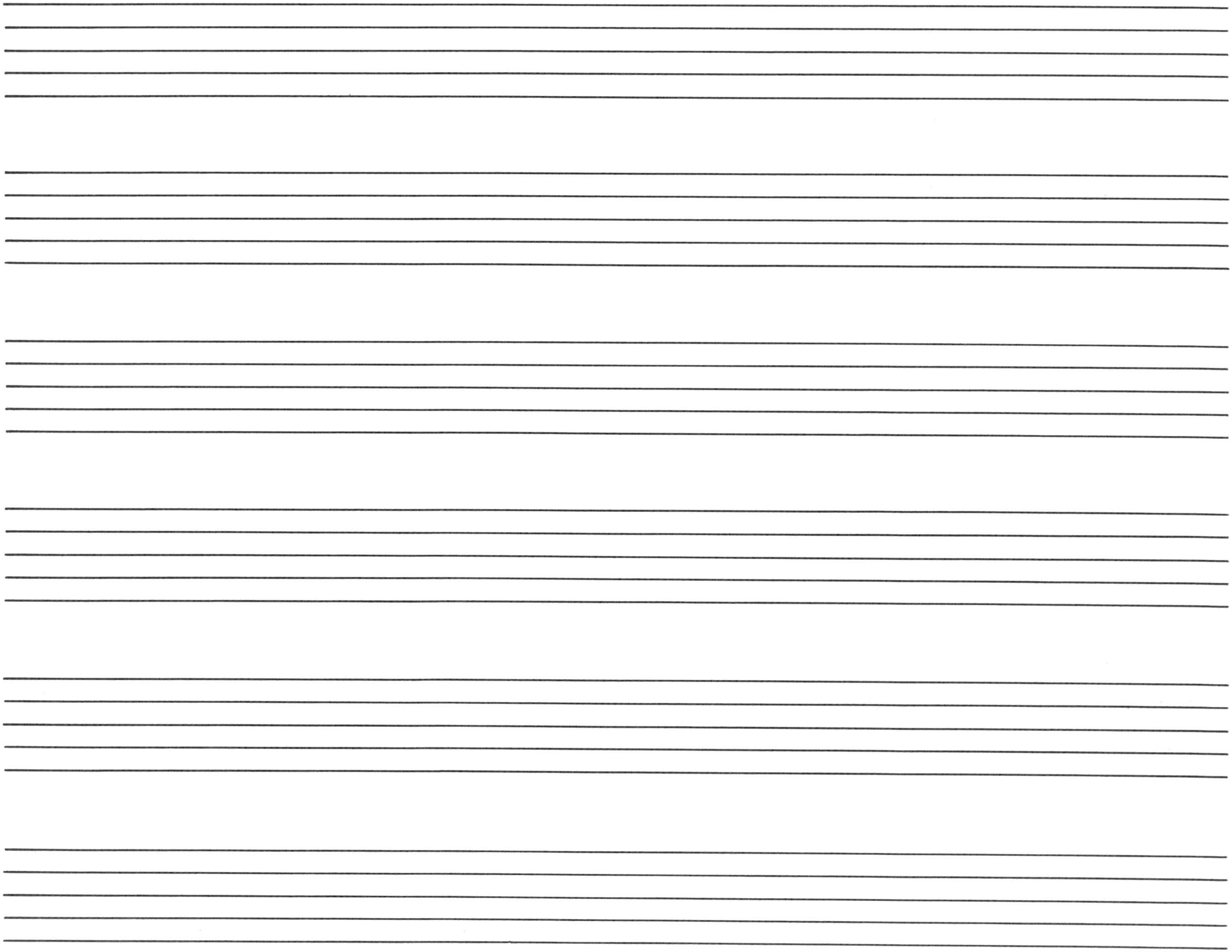

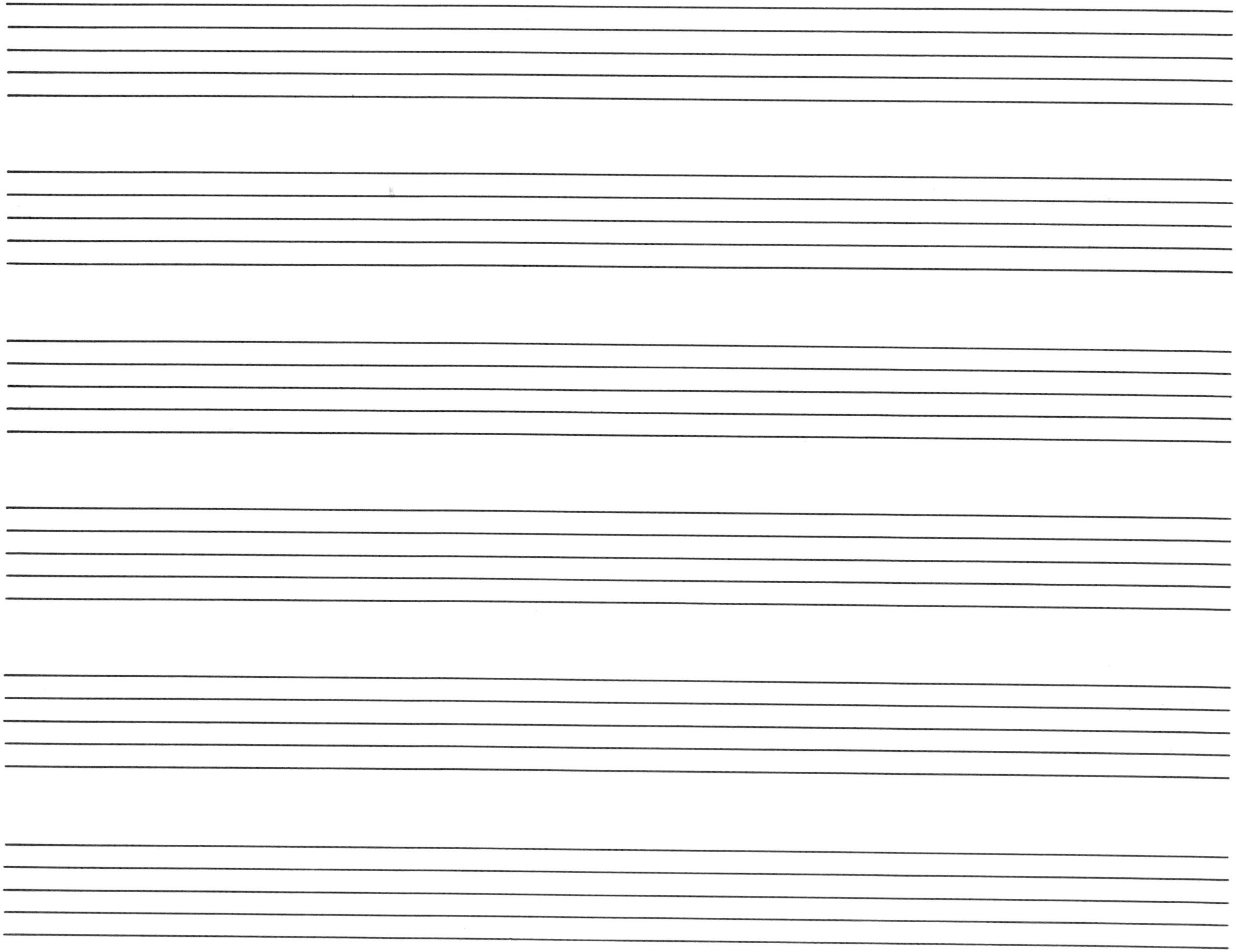

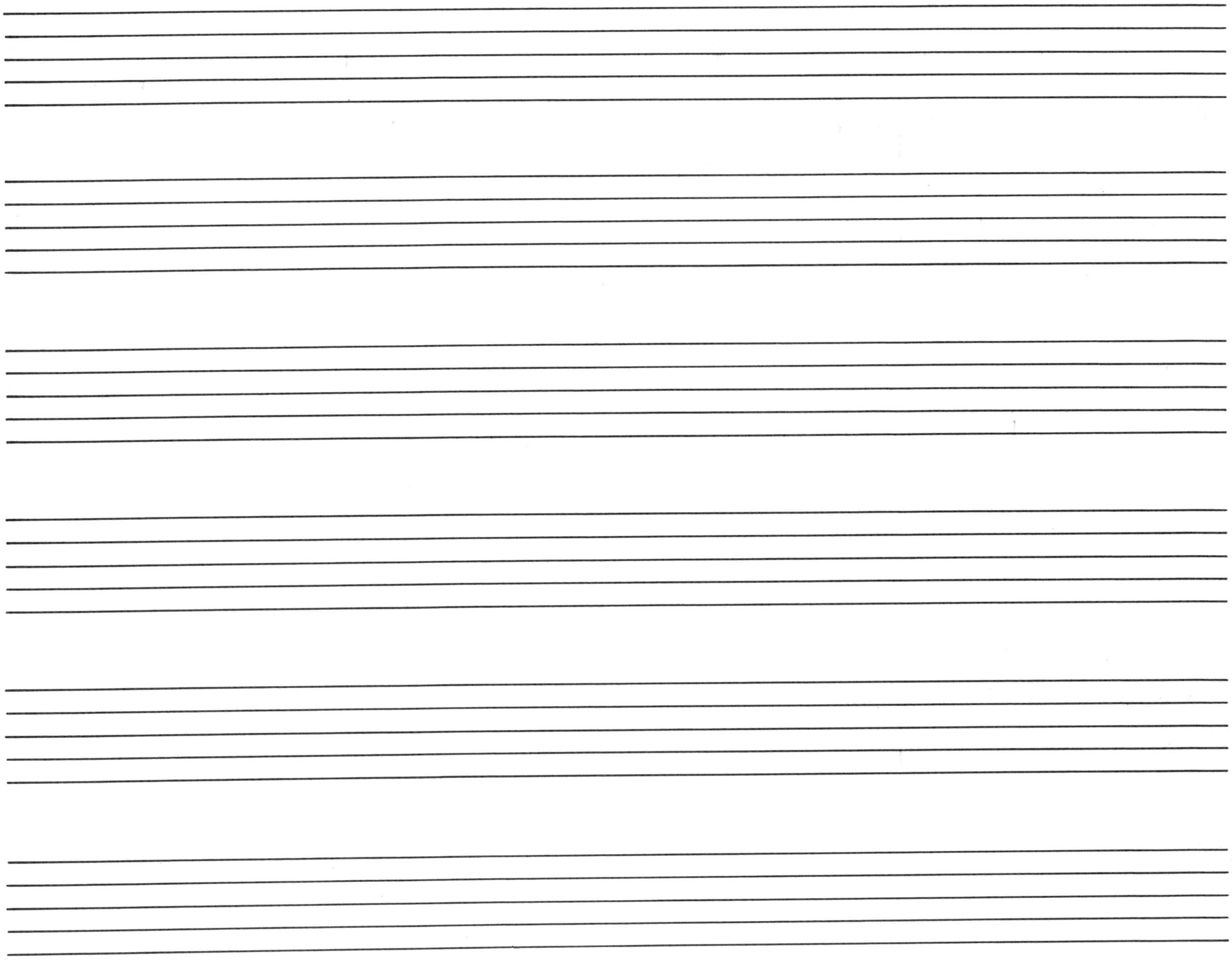

Grand Staff Treble + Bass Clef Together

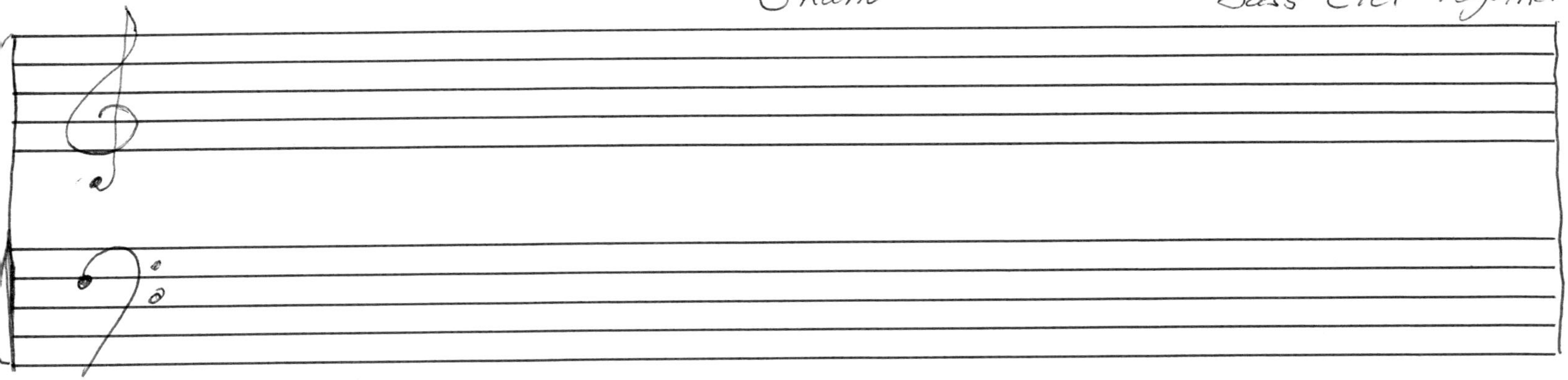

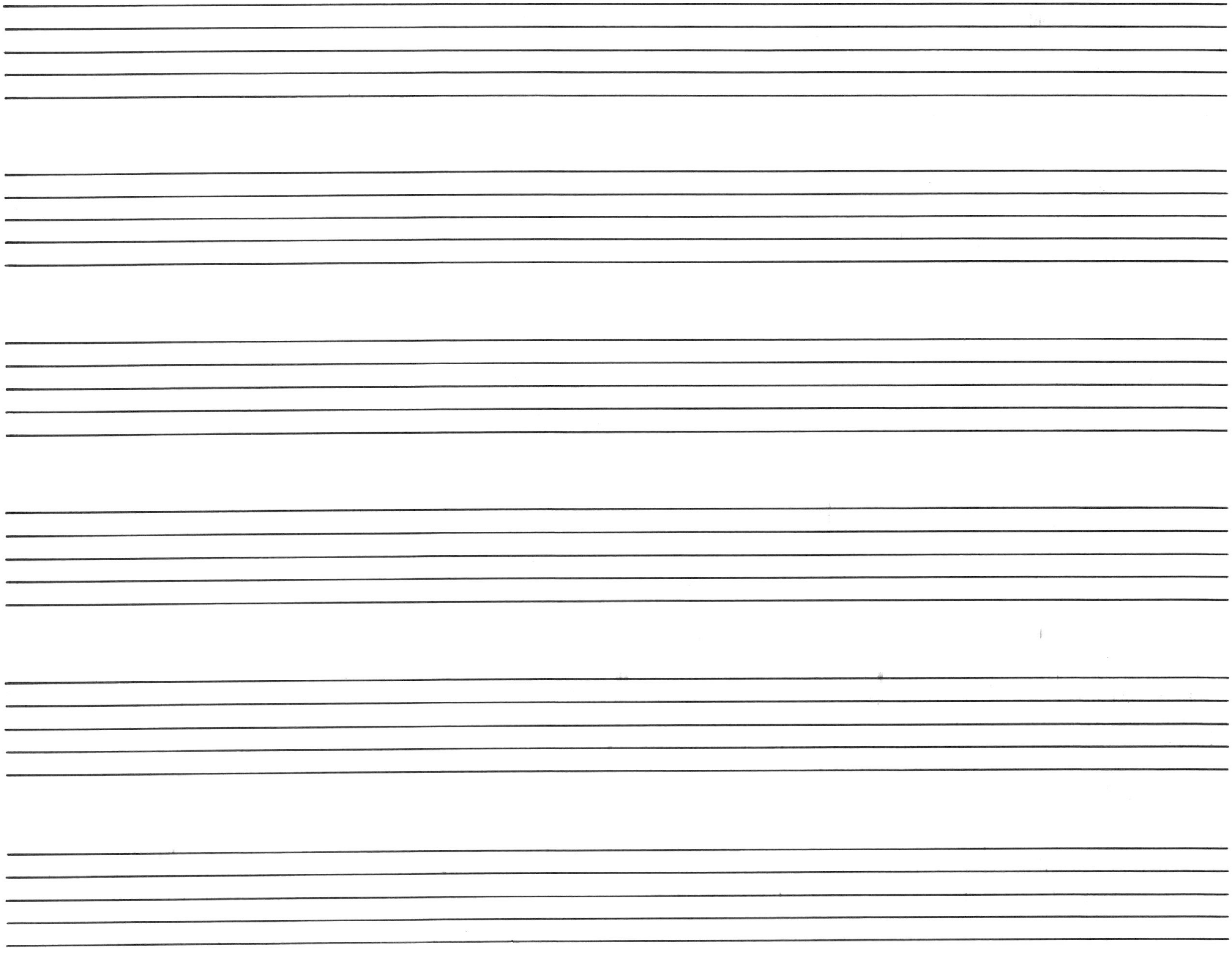

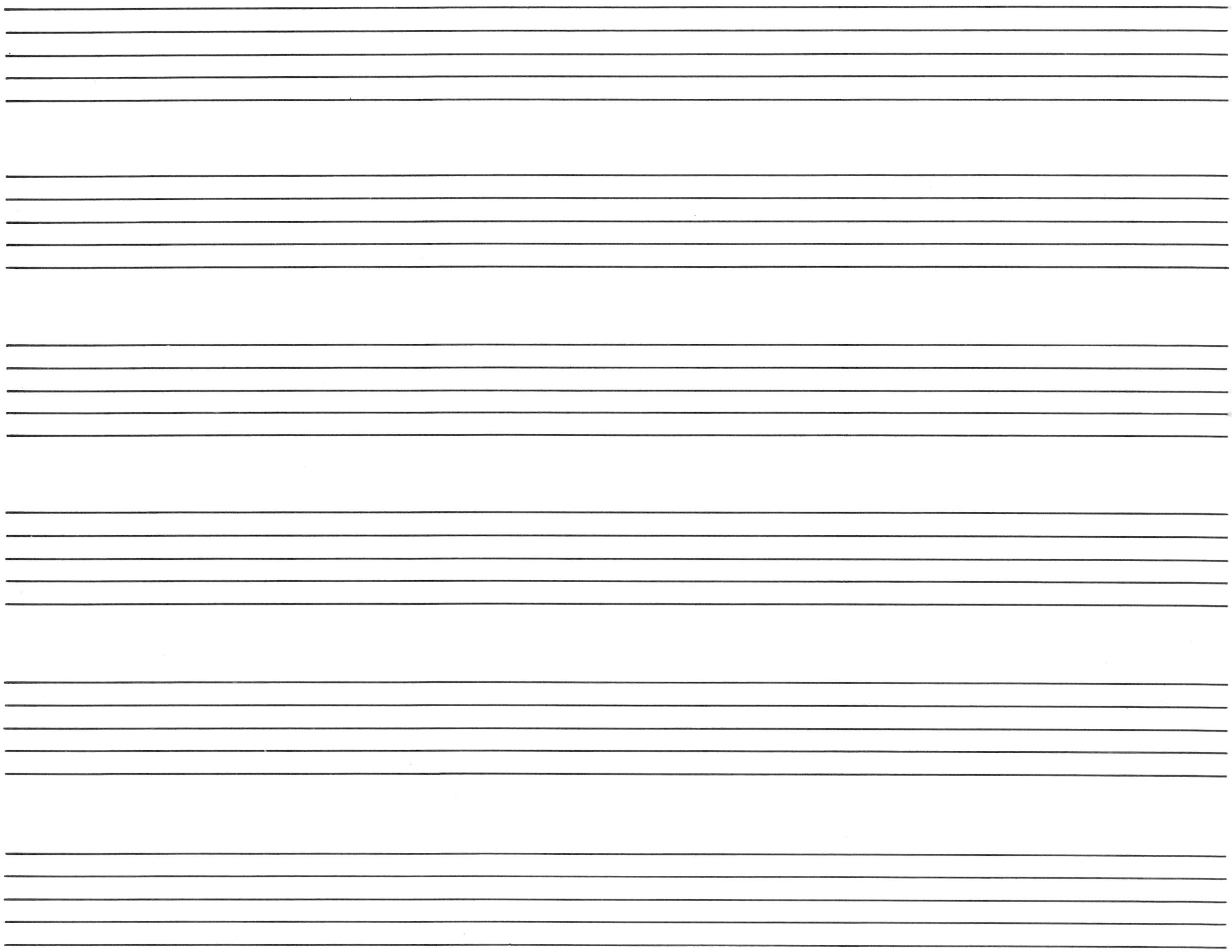